Embracing the Future:

Navigating the World of Remote Work and Hybrid Models

Richard R. Alexander

Table of Contents

The Evolution of Remote Work:

A Look Back at its Rise During the Pandemic and Prospects for Hybrid Models.

Introduction:

The evolution of remote work has been a remarkable journey, accelerated by the unprecedented events of the COVID-19 pandemic. Before the pandemic, remote work was a relatively niche concept, limited to certain industries and job roles. However, the pandemic forced businesses and employees worldwide to adapt rapidly, leading to an exponential rise in remote work adoption. As the world moves forward in 2023, remote work has become a well-established and accepted way of conducting business. This article examines the key milestones in the evolution of remote work, how it rose during the pandemic, and the prospects for hybrid models in the current landscape.

1. Early Adoption of Remote Work:

Before the pandemic, remote work was more commonly practiced in tech-centric industries, freelancing, and certain progressive companies. It was often seen as a perk rather than a standard work arrangement. Early adopters of remote work valued its potential to increase employee satisfaction, reduce commuting time, and tap into a global talent pool.

2. The Pandemic Catalyst:

The COVID-19 pandemic struck the world in early 2020, forcing governments to implement lockdowns and social distancing measures. In response, businesses had no choice but to pivot to remote work to continue their operations. The transition was not without challenges, as many companies had to rapidly upgrade their infrastructure, provide employees with necessary tools, and address concerns about productivity and work-life balance.

3. The Rise of Remote Work During the Pandemic:

During the pandemic, remote work experienced an unparalleled surge. Companies across all sectors, even those that were traditionally office-based, shifted to remote work models. Employees adapted to video conferencing tools, cloud-based collaboration platforms, and remote project management systems. Many organizations found that their employees could maintain productivity levels, leading to a shift in attitudes towards remote work as a viable long-term solution.

4. Advantages of Remote Work:

As the pandemic unfolded, businesses and employees discovered several advantages of remote work. These included:

- **Flexibility:** Employees appreciated the ability to set their own schedules and work from different locations, leading to better work-life balance.

- **Cost Savings:** Businesses could reduce overhead costs associated with office space, utilities, and other office-related expenses.

- **Access to Global Talent:** Remote work allowed companies to hire the best talent from around the world, unrestricted by geographical boundaries.

- **Resilience:** Remote work enabled businesses to continue operations during emergencies and natural disasters.

5. Challenges of Remote Work:

While remote work proved to be beneficial, it also came with its own set of challenges, such as:

- **Digital Divide:** Disparities in access to technology and reliable internet connections affected some employees' ability to work remotely effectively.

- **Social Isolation:** Employees missed the social interactions and camaraderie of the office environment, impacting team dynamics and employee well-being.

- **Communication and Collaboration:** Virtual

communication tools couldn't fully replicate the spontaneity and effectiveness of face-to-face interactions.

- **Work-Life Balance:** Blurring boundaries between work and personal life led to potential burnout and mental health issues for some employees.

6. The Hybrid Work Model in 2023:

As the pandemic subsided and the world adjusted to new norms, a hybrid work model emerged as a popular solution for many organizations. In the hybrid model, employees split their time between working remotely and going into the office. This approach aimed to combine the benefits of remote work with the advantages of in-person collaboration.

7. Prospects for Hybrid Work:

The hybrid work model is expected to become the dominant work arrangement in 2023 for several reasons:

- **Flexibility and Customization:** Hybrid models allow companies to tailor their approach based on their industry, company culture, and employee preferences.

- **Talent Attraction and Retention:** Offering a hybrid work option can attract top talent who value flexibility and empower companies to retain experienced employees.

- **Reduced Office Space:** Companies can downsize their office spaces, reducing costs while still maintaining a physical presence for team meetings and collaboration.

- **Environmental Impact:** With reduced commuting, hybrid work can contribute to lower carbon emissions and support sustainability efforts.

Conclusion:

The evolution of remote work from a niche practice to a mainstream work arrangement has been transformative. The pandemic accelerated this evolution, leading to widespread adoption and acceptance of remote work. In 2023, the hybrid work model is set to redefine the way we work, combining the best elements of remote work with the benefits of in-person collaboration. The future of work is likely to be a dynamic blend of physical and virtual spaces, empowering both businesses and employees to thrive in the post-pandemic world.

Advantages and Challenges of Remote Work:

Lessons Learned from the Pandemic and How Hybrid Models Address Them.

Advantages of Remote Work:

1. Flexibility and Work-Life Balance: Remote work allows employees to have more control over their schedules, leading to improved work-life balance. They can adapt their work hours to personal needs, resulting in higher job satisfaction and reduced stress.

2. Cost Savings: For both employees and employers, remote work can lead to cost savings. Employees save money on commuting, work attire, and meals, while employers can reduce expenses related to office space and utilities.

3. **Access to a Global Talent Pool:** Remote work enables companies to hire talent from anywhere in the world. This expanded talent pool allows businesses to access specialized skills and diverse perspectives that might not be available locally.

4. **Increased Productivity:** Many employees report higher productivity levels when working remotely. Fewer distractions, reduced office politics, and a personalized work environment contribute to improved focus and output.

5. **Business Continuity and Resilience:** Remote work proved to be invaluable during the pandemic, as it allowed companies to continue operating despite office closures and lockdowns. Having a remote work infrastructure in place enhances a

company's resilience during emergencies and unforeseen disruptions.

Challenges of Remote Work:

1. **Digital Divide:** Remote work relies heavily on technology, but not all employees have equal access to reliable internet connections and necessary devices. This digital divide can hinder the productivity of certain individuals and create inequities in the workforce.

2. **Isolation and Communication Issues:** Remote work can lead to feelings of isolation, particularly for employees who thrive on social interactions. Virtual communication may also suffer from misinterpretations and lack of real-time feedback, affecting team dynamics and collaboration.

3. **Maintaining Work-Life Boundaries:** When work and home environments merge,

it becomes challenging for employees to establish clear boundaries between their personal and professional lives. This can lead to burnout and decreased overall well-being.

4. **Team Building and Company Culture:** Building a strong team and fostering company culture can be more challenging in a remote setting. Casual interactions and spontaneous discussions that contribute to a cohesive team dynamic are more difficult to replicate virtually.

How Hybrid Models Address the Challenges:

1. **Flexibility with In-Person Collaboration:** Hybrid models offer the best of both worlds by allowing employees to work remotely part of the time and come into the office for specific periods. This setup ensures flexibility while still providing

opportunities for in-person interactions and team building.

2. Mitigating the Digital Divide: Employers adopting hybrid models can invest in resources and support for employees who face digital divide challenges. This could include providing hardware, reimbursing internet costs, or offering access to co-working spaces.

3. Balancing Work-Life Boundaries: Hybrid models enable employees to set dedicated work-from-home days and office days, helping them create a clear separation between their personal and professional lives. This can promote a healthier work-life balance.

4. Enhancing Communication and Collaboration: Hybrid models encourage companies to optimize their communication strategies. This might involve using digital collaboration tools effectively for remote work and fostering regular in-person meetings for team bonding and brainstorming sessions.

5. **Empowering Employee Choice:** Hybrid models empower employees to choose the work environment that suits them best for specific tasks. For some, creative tasks might be better accomplished in a remote, distraction-free setting, while collaborative projects benefit from in-person brainstorming sessions.

6. **Adapting Company Culture:** With a hybrid model, companies can create a flexible company culture that accommodates both remote and in-office employees. Regular team-building events, workshops, and social gatherings can be organized to foster a cohesive team despite the physical distance.

Conclusion:

The advantages of remote work, such as increased flexibility and access to a global talent pool, are undeniable. However, the challenges it poses, like the digital divide and communication issues, cannot be overlooked. Hybrid work models have emerged as a strategic response to address these challenges while leveraging the benefits of remote work and in-person collaboration. By implementing well-thought-out hybrid models, companies can optimize productivity, employee satisfaction, and business resilience in a post-pandemic world.

Managing Remote Teams Effectively:

Best Practices for Communication, Collaboration, and Productivity.

Managing remote teams effectively is crucial for ensuring productivity, maintaining team cohesion, and achieving organizational goals. Remote work presents unique challenges, but with the right strategies and best practices, you can foster a successful remote work environment. Here are some key practices for managing remote teams effectively:

1. Clear Communication:

- **Use the Right Tools:** Invest in reliable communication and collaboration tools, such as video conferencing, instant messaging, and project management platforms. Ensure that all team members have access to these tools and are comfortable using them.

- **Establish Communication Norms:** Set clear expectations for how and when team members should communicate. Define response times for emails and messages to avoid delays and confusion.

- **Encourage Regular Check-ins:** Schedule regular team meetings and one-on-one check-ins to discuss progress, challenges, and updates. These meetings foster a sense of connection and keep everyone aligned.

- **Be Transparent:** Keep the team informed about important decisions, company updates, and project changes. Transparency builds trust among team members and enhances collaboration.

2. Promote Collaboration:

- **Virtual Brainstorming Sessions:** Conduct virtual brainstorming sessions to encourage creative thinking and problem-solving. Use collaboration tools that allow real-time contributions from all team members.

- **Encourage Knowledge Sharing:** Create a culture of knowledge sharing within the team. Use platforms like shared documents or wikis to centralize information and resources.

- **Promote Team Building Activities:** Organize virtual team-building activities to foster camaraderie and strengthen interpersonal bonds. These activities could include virtual games, online workshops, or social events.

- **Cross-Functional Collaboration:** Encourage collaboration between different departments or teams. Cross-functional projects can lead to innovative solutions and a deeper understanding of the organization's overall goals.

3. Set Clear Goals and Expectations:

- **Define Measurable Objectives:** Establish clear, measurable goals for each team member and the team as a whole. This clarity helps track progress and ensures everyone is aligned with the organization's objectives.

- **Individual Accountability:** Clearly communicate each team member's responsibilities and deadlines. Hold individuals accountable for their tasks while providing support and resources as needed.

- **Flexibility with Schedules:** Acknowledge that remote team members may have different working hours due to various time zones or personal preferences. Focus on results rather than rigid working hours.

4. Foster a Positive Team Culture:

- **Recognition and Appreciation:** Recognize and appreciate team members' efforts and achievements. Celebrate successes, milestones, and contributions publicly to boost morale.

- **Encourage Feedback:** Create a culture of open feedback, where team members can share ideas, concerns, and suggestions without fear of judgment. Regularly solicit feedback from the team to identify areas for improvement.

- **Promote Work-Life Balance:** Encourage work-life balance by respecting boundaries and promoting self-care. Offer flexibility when needed and discourage overworking.

5. Provide Professional Development Opportunities:

- **Skill Development:** Support team members' professional growth by offering training opportunities, webinars, or workshops related to their roles and career aspirations.

- **Mentorship and Coaching:** Pair experienced team members with less experienced ones for mentorship. Provide coaching and guidance to help team members overcome challenges and develop their skills.

Conclusion:

Managing remote teams effectively requires a strong emphasis on clear communication, fostering collaboration, setting clear goals, and nurturing a positive team culture. By implementing these best practices, you can create a productive and engaged remote team that achieves success and maintains a sense of camaraderie despite physical distances. Flexibility, adaptability, and a supportive approach are essential elements in successfully managing remote teams in today's dynamic work environment.

Building a Thriving Hybrid Work Culture:

Fostering Team Cohesion and Inclusivity Across Distributed Locations.

Building a thriving hybrid work culture is essential for ensuring team cohesion, maintaining inclusivity, and maximizing productivity across distributed locations. A hybrid work environment combines both remote and in-office work, allowing employees to work from different locations based on their preferences and job requirements. Here are the key strategies to foster a thriving hybrid work culture:

1. Communication and Transparency:

- **Consistent Communication Channels:** Establish regular

communication channels for both remote and in-office employees. Use video conferencing, instant messaging, and collaboration tools to ensure everyone stays connected.

- **All-Hands Meetings:** Organize regular all-hands meetings where the entire team gathers virtually. Share important updates, company goals, and celebrate achievements to foster a sense of belonging.

- **Transparency in Decision-Making:** Keep the decision-making process transparent and involve all team members in discussions when appropriate. Transparency builds trust and ensures inclusivity.

2. Inclusivity and Equity:

- **Equal Opportunities:** Ensure that remote and in-office employees have equal access to growth opportunities, promotions, and recognition. Avoid favoritism or bias in assignments and decision-making.

- **Include Remote Team Members:** Proactively involve remote employees in team activities and social events. Consider time zones when scheduling events to accommodate all team members.

- **Encourage Collaboration:** Set the expectation that remote and in-office team members collaborate equally. Avoid any division between the two groups and foster a united team spirit.

3. Flexible Work Policies:

- **Customizable Schedules:** Offer flexible work hours and remote work options to suit individual preferences and needs. Empower employees to tailor their schedules for maximum productivity.

- **Hybrid Work Guidelines:** Develop clear policies and guidelines for the hybrid work model. Communicate expectations regarding office days, remote work arrangements, and communication protocols.

- **Trial Period and Feedback:** Implement a trial period for the hybrid work model and gather feedback from employees to assess its effectiveness and make necessary adjustments.

4. Team-Building Activities:

- **Virtual Team-Building:** Plan regular virtual team-building activities that involve both remote and in-office employees. Virtual games, online workshops, and collaborative projects can promote team cohesion.

- **In-Person Gatherings:** Organize periodic in-person team-building events or retreats when feasible and safe. These events provide valuable opportunities for team bonding and relationship-building.

5. Collaboration and Knowledge Sharing:

- **Collaboration Tools:** Invest in effective collaboration tools that facilitate seamless communication and file sharing among team members, regardless of their location.

- **Centralized Knowledge Base:**
Create a centralized knowledge base or document repository accessible to all team members. This helps streamline information sharing and avoids silos.

- **Encourage Cross-Functional Collaboration:** Promote collaboration across different departments or teams to foster a culture of shared knowledge and mutual support.

6. Focus on Results and Performance:

- **Outcome-Based Assessment:**
Shift the focus from monitoring working hours to measuring results and performance. Set clear performance metrics and celebrate achievements.

- **Regular Performance Reviews:** Conduct regular performance reviews that provide constructive feedback and support employees in achieving their goals.

Conclusion:

Building a thriving hybrid work culture requires intentional efforts to foster team cohesion, promote inclusivity, and enable seamless collaboration across distributed locations. Effective communication, transparent decision-making, and equitable opportunities are essential components of such a culture. By embracing flexibility, encouraging team-building activities, and leveraging technology for collaboration, organizations can create an environment where all team members feel valued, connected, and empowered to thrive in the hybrid work landscape.

Productivity in a Hybrid Work Environment:

Strategies to Boost Efficiency and Accountability.

Productivity in a hybrid work environment can be optimized through the implementation of specific strategies that promote efficiency, collaboration, and accountability. In a hybrid work setup, where employees split their time between remote and in-office work, maintaining productivity requires a balance between flexibility and structure. Here are some strategies to boost productivity in a hybrid work environment:

1. Clearly Define Goals and Expectations:

- **Set Clear Objectives:** Clearly communicate the organization's goals and individual team member's objectives. Ensure that everyone understands their role in achieving these goals.

- **SMART Goals:** Encourage the setting of Specific, Measurable, Achievable, Relevant, and Time-bound (SMART) goals for each project or task. This helps employees stay focused and motivated.

2. Establish Flexible Work Schedules:

- **Customizable Work Hours:** Offer flexibility in work hours, allowing employees to choose their most productive time for certain tasks. This accommodates individual preferences and work styles.

- **Core Hours:** Establish core hours when all team members are expected to be available for collaboration and communication. This helps facilitate teamwork and avoids communication gaps.

3. Leverage Collaboration Tools:

- **Effective Communication Platforms:** Utilize video conferencing, instant messaging, and project management tools to facilitate seamless communication among team members, regardless of their location.

- **Cloud-Based Collaboration:** Adopt cloud-based platforms for file sharing and collaborative document editing, enabling real-time updates and reducing version control issues.

4. Implement Regular Check-ins and Feedback:

- **Scheduled Team Meetings:** Hold regular team meetings to discuss progress, address challenges, and provide updates on projects. Virtual meetings should be inclusive of both remote and in-office employees.

- **One-on-One Check-ins:** Conduct one-on-one meetings with each team member to provide personalized feedback, offer support, and address any concerns they may have.

5. Encourage Employee Autonomy:

- **Empower Decision-Making:** Encourage employees to make autonomous decisions within their areas of expertise. This sense of ownership can increase motivation and accountability.

- **Results-Oriented Approach:** Focus on outcomes rather than micromanaging the process. Trust employees to achieve their goals and reward them for their achievements.

6. Foster Team Collaboration:

- **Hybrid Team-Building Activities:** Organize team-building activities that involve both remote and in-office employees. This fosters a sense of camaraderie and strengthens team dynamics.

- **Cross-Functional Projects:** Encourage collaboration between different departments or teams on projects, promoting knowledge sharing and a broader understanding of the organization.

7. Provide Training and Skill Development:

- **Continuous Learning:** Invest in training and skill development opportunities to enhance employees' capabilities and keep them up-to-date with industry trends.

- **Upskilling for Remote Work:** Offer training programs that focus on building skills essential for remote work, such as time management, remote communication, and self-motivation.

8. Recognize and Celebrate Achievements:

- **Appreciation and Recognition:** Acknowledge employees' efforts and accomplishments regularly. Recognize their contributions publicly to boost morale and motivation.

- **Celebrating Milestones:** Celebrate project milestones and successful outcomes with the entire team, promoting a positive and supportive work culture.

9. Measure and Adjust:

- **Performance Metrics:** Establish key performance indicators (KPIs) to measure individual and team productivity. Regularly assess progress and use the data to identify areas for improvement.

- **Flexibility for Improvement:** Be open to making adjustments and improvements based on feedback from employees and performance assessments.

Conclusion:

Boosting productivity in a hybrid work environment requires a combination of clear communication, collaboration tools, flexible work schedules, and a results-oriented approach. Encouraging autonomy, fostering collaboration, providing training, and recognizing achievements are essential for creating a productive and thriving hybrid work culture. Regularly assess the effectiveness of implemented strategies and be willing to adapt to the changing needs of the workforce in order to achieve sustained productivity in the hybrid work landscape.

Work-Life Balance in Remote and Hybrid Models:

Creating Boundaries and Avoiding Burnout.

Work-life balance is crucial for employee well-being and productivity in both remote and hybrid work models. While these models offer flexibility and autonomy, they can also blur the lines between work and personal life, leading to burnout and decreased job satisfaction. Here are strategies to create boundaries and maintain work-life balance in remote and hybrid work environments:

1. Set Clear Work Hours and Boundaries:

- **Establish Consistent Hours:** Define regular work hours and stick to them as much as possible. Consistency helps maintain a routine and separates work from personal time.

- **Communicate Boundaries:** Communicate your work hours and availability to your team and colleagues. Respect your personal time and avoid responding to work-related messages outside of designated hours.

2. Designate a Dedicated Workspace:

- **Create a Productive Environment:** Set up a dedicated workspace at home or in the office that promotes focus and productivity. Keep it organized and free from distractions.

- **Physically and Mentally Disconnect:** When you leave your workspace, mentally disengage from work-related thoughts. This separation helps you transition into personal time.

3. Take Regular Breaks:

- **Schedule Breaks:** Incorporate regular breaks into your workday to recharge and avoid burnout. Step away from your desk, stretch, or engage in a quick physical activity.

- **Encourage Micro-breaks:** Encourage short, frequent breaks during prolonged tasks to maintain focus and prevent fatigue.

4. Prioritize Self-Care:

- **Schedule Personal Activities:** Set aside time for personal hobbies, exercise, or relaxation. Treat these activities as non-negotiable commitments.

- **Practice Mindfulness:** Incorporate mindfulness techniques, such as meditation or deep breathing exercises, to reduce stress and increase focus.

5. Communicate Work-Life Needs:

- **Open Dialogue with Managers:** If you are facing challenges with work-life balance, discuss your needs and concerns with your manager. Open communication can lead to reasonable accommodations.

- **Set Expectations with Family and Friends:** Communicate your work schedule and commitments to family and friends, so they understand your availability and support your boundaries.

6. Time Management and Prioritization:

- **Set Clear Goals:** Define your daily and weekly goals to prioritize tasks effectively. Focus on completing high-priority tasks during your most productive hours.

- **Avoid Overcommitment:** Be mindful of taking on too many tasks. Learn to say no when necessary to maintain a manageable workload.

7. Implement "Work from Anywhere" Policies:

- **Explore Remote Work Opportunities:** Embrace the flexibility of remote work by occasionally working from different locations, such as co-working spaces or coffee shops. Change of scenery can be refreshing.

- **Travel and Remote Work:** If your company allows it, consider combining travel with remote work to experience new environments without sacrificing productivity.

8. Encourage Time Off and Vacation:

- **Use Vacation Days:** Take advantage of your allocated vacation days to fully disconnect from work and recharge.

- **Support Employee Time Off:** Managers should encourage and support employees in taking their vacation days without feeling guilty or anxious about work piling up.

9. Regularly Assess Work-Life Balance:

- **Self-Reflection:** Regularly assess your work-life balance and make adjustments as needed. Identify patterns of burnout or stress and take action to address them.

- **Organizational Support:** Employers should conduct surveys and check-ins to gauge employee work-life balance and offer resources or support if needed.

Conclusion:

Work-life balance is achievable in both remote and hybrid work models through a combination of setting clear boundaries, time management, prioritization, and self-care. Open communication with managers and colleagues, along with regular assessments of work-life balance, are vital for maintaining employee well-being and preventing burnout. By fostering a culture that values work-life balance, organizations can promote a healthier and more productive workforce in the evolving work landscape.

The Role of Technology in Remote Work and Hybrid Models:

Tools for Seamless Collaboration and Connectivity.

The role of technology in remote work and hybrid models is critical for enabling seamless collaboration, ensuring connectivity, and supporting productivity across distributed teams. Advancements in technology have revolutionized the way we work, making remote work and hybrid models more feasible and efficient than ever before. Here are some key aspects of technology's role in these work models:

1. Communication Tools:

- **Video Conferencing:** Platforms like Zoom, Microsoft Teams, and Google Meet facilitate face-to-face virtual meetings, enabling teams to communicate effectively, regardless of physical distance.

- **Instant Messaging:** Tools like Slack and Microsoft Teams provide real-time messaging, fostering quick and efficient communication among team members.

- **Email:** While considered traditional, email remains a crucial communication tool for sharing formal documents, announcements, and important updates.

2. Cloud-Based Collaboration:

- **File Sharing and Storage:** Cloud storage services like Google Drive, Dropbox, and Microsoft OneDrive allow teams to share and access files from any location, promoting collaboration on documents, presentations, and projects.

- **Collaborative Editing:** Cloud-based office suites like Google Workspace and Microsoft Office 365 enable multiple team members to work on the same document simultaneously, streamlining the editing process.

- **Version Control:** Cloud-based collaboration tools offer version history, ensuring that the latest changes are saved, and previous versions can be accessed if needed.

3. Project Management Platforms:

- **Task Assignment and Tracking:** Project management tools like Trello, Asana, and Jira help teams assign tasks, set deadlines, and track progress on projects, ensuring accountability and visibility.

- **Gantt Charts:** Gantt chart-based tools provide a visual representation of project timelines, helping teams plan and manage complex projects efficiently.

4. Virtual Whiteboards and Brainstorming:

- **Virtual Whiteboards:** Tools like Miro and MURAL enable remote teams to collaborate on visual brainstorming sessions, idea mapping, and creative problem-solving.

- **Mind Mapping Software:** Applications like XMind and MindMeister facilitate the creation of mind maps for organizing ideas and concepts.

5. Virtual Training and Onboarding:

- **E-Learning Platforms:** Companies can use e-learning platforms like Udemy, Coursera, and LinkedIn Learning to provide remote training and skill development for employees.

- **Virtual Onboarding:** Virtual onboarding platforms and tools make it possible to onboard and integrate new employees into the company remotely.

6. Security and Data Protection:

- **VPN (Virtual Private Network):** VPNs enhance security by creating a secure and encrypted connection between remote employees and the company's internal network.

- **Multi-Factor Authentication (MFA):** MFA adds an extra layer of security by requiring users to provide multiple forms of identification to access sensitive information and systems.

7. Remote IT Support:

- **Remote Desktop Software:** IT support teams can use remote desktop software like TeamViewer and AnyDesk to access employees' computers remotely and troubleshoot issues.

- **Helpdesk Software:** Helpdesk tools like Zendesk and Freshdesk provide efficient ticketing systems for tracking and resolving IT-related requests.

8. Connectivity and Network Infrastructure:

- **Reliable Internet Connections:** Remote and hybrid work models depend heavily on reliable internet connectivity to ensure smooth communication and collaboration.

- **Wireless Networks and Hardware:** Employers should provide remote employees with necessary hardware, such as routers and printers, to create a stable and productive work environment.

Conclusion:

Technology plays a fundamental role in enabling remote work and hybrid models by providing tools for seamless collaboration, communication, and connectivity. From video conferencing to cloud-based collaboration and project management platforms, technology empowers teams to work efficiently, regardless of their physical location. Embracing the right technology and supporting remote employees with the necessary tools and infrastructure are essential for creating a successful and productive remote work culture in the modern workplace.

Bridging the Gap:

Overcoming Communication Challenges in Hybrid Teams.

Bridging the gap and overcoming communication challenges in hybrid teams is crucial for ensuring effective collaboration, maintaining team cohesion, and maximizing productivity. In hybrid teams, where some members work remotely and others are in the office, communication barriers can arise due to differences in work locations, time zones, and communication preferences.

Here are strategies to address these challenges and foster seamless communication in hybrid teams:

1. Implement a Communication Protocol:

- **Clear Guidelines:** Establish clear communication guidelines that outline preferred communication channels, response times, and appropriate use of each platform.

- **Consistency:** Encourage consistent communication practices to create a predictable and reliable communication environment for all team members.

2. Leverage Technology for Virtual Collaboration:

- **Video Conferencing:** Use video conferencing tools for team meetings, project discussions, and brainstorming sessions to facilitate face-to-face interactions despite physical distances.

- **Instant Messaging:** Adopt real-time messaging platforms to enable quick, informal communication and maintain connectivity throughout the workday.

- **Project Management Tools:** Utilize project management software to assign tasks, track progress, and centralize project-related discussions.

3. Set Core Hours for Collaboration:

- **Overlap Hours:** Identify core working hours when all team members are available for collaboration and synchronous communication. This overlap helps address time zone differences.

- **Flexibility:** Allow for some flexibility in core hours to accommodate individual preferences and personal commitments.

4. Encourage Active Participation:

- **Equal Opportunities:** Ensure that both remote and in-office team members have equal opportunities to contribute in meetings and discussions.

- **Encourage Input:** Create an inclusive environment that encourages all team members to share their ideas, perspectives, and concerns.

5. Promote Face-to-Face Interactions:

- **In-Person Meetings:** When possible, arrange periodic in-person meetings or team-building events to foster stronger interpersonal relationships.

- **Hybrid Team-Building Activities:** Organize virtual team-building activities that involve both remote and in-office employees to build camaraderie.

6. Provide Training on Remote Communication:

- **Virtual Communication Skills:** Offer training on effective virtual communication, including active listening, concise messaging, and clear articulation.

- **Cultural Awareness:** Sensitize team members to cultural differences that may impact communication styles and norms.

7. Foster a Culture of Feedback:

- **Regular Feedback:** Encourage regular feedback among team members to identify and address communication challenges and improve collaboration.

- **Openness to Suggestions:**
  Demonstrate openness to suggestions
  and improvements in the team's
  communication practices.

8. Emphasize Documentation and Transparency:

- **Document Meetings and
  Decisions:** Record key points and
  decisions from meetings to ensure
  everyone is on the same page,
  especially for remote team members
  who might miss in-person discussions.

- **Transparency in
  Communication:** Be transparent
  with important updates, changes, and
  decisions to avoid misunderstandings
  and promote trust.

9. Monitor and Adjust Communication Strategies:

- **Continuous Improvement:** Regularly assess the effectiveness of communication strategies and make adjustments based on feedback and evolving needs.

- **Regular Check-ins:** Conduct periodic check-ins with team members to evaluate their communication experiences and make necessary improvements.

Conclusion:

Effective communication is the cornerstone of success in hybrid teams. By implementing clear guidelines, leveraging technology, promoting active participation, and fostering a culture of feedback and transparency, teams can overcome communication challenges and bridge the gap between remote and in-office team members. Embracing a proactive approach to communication in hybrid teams will lead to better collaboration, enhanced team cohesion, and improved overall productivity.

Nurturing Employee Engagement in a Hybrid Workforce:

Keeping Remote and In-Office Employees Connected.

Nurturing employee engagement in a hybrid workforce is crucial for creating a cohesive and productive team environment. With remote and in-office employees working together, it's essential to bridge the gap and foster a sense of connection and belonging. Here are strategies to keep remote and in-office employees connected and engaged in a hybrid work environment:

1. Build a Strong Company Culture:

- **Clear Company Values:** Clearly communicate the company's values and mission to all employees, regardless of their location. A strong company culture helps foster a shared sense of purpose and identity.

- **Inclusive Culture:** Create an inclusive culture that celebrates diversity and ensures all team members feel valued and respected.

2. Encourage Regular Communication:

- **Virtual Team Meetings:** Conduct regular virtual team meetings to provide updates, share successes, and promote open discussions. Ensure remote employees are included and have opportunities to contribute.

- **One-on-One Check-Ins:** Managers should schedule regular one-on-one check-ins with both remote and in-office employees to offer support, provide feedback, and address any concerns.

3. Foster Virtual Collaboration:

- **Virtual Brainstorming Sessions:** Conduct virtual brainstorming sessions to involve remote employees in ideation and decision-making processes.

- **Collaborative Tools:** Utilize collaborative software and project management platforms to encourage teamwork and information sharing across the team.

4. Virtual Team-Building Activities:

- **Remote Social Events:** Organize virtual team-building activities and social events that allow remote and in-office employees to interact and bond.

- **Virtual Games and Competitions:** Plan fun virtual games and competitions that promote team spirit and friendly competition among all employees.

5. Provide Training and Skill Development:

- **Virtual Training Opportunities:** Offer remote employees access to virtual training and development programs to enhance their skills and career growth.

- **Cross-Training:** Encourage cross-training opportunities between remote and in-office employees to foster knowledge sharing and collaboration.

6. Recognize and Appreciate Contributions:

- **Regular Recognition:** Recognize and appreciate employees' efforts and achievements publicly, ensuring remote employees are acknowledged and celebrated.

- **Rewards and Incentives:** Offer rewards and incentives for outstanding performance, regardless of the employee's work location.

7. Flexibility and Work-Life Balance:

- **Empower Flexibility:** Provide flexibility in work hours and location, enabling employees to balance their personal and professional responsibilities effectively.

- **Respect Work-Life Boundaries:** Encourage managers and colleagues to respect employees' work-life boundaries, regardless of their location.

8. Support Wellness and Mental Health:

- **Employee Assistance Programs (EAP):** Offer employee assistance programs that provide resources for mental health support and wellness.

- **Wellness Initiatives:** Implement wellness initiatives that cater to both remote and in-office employees, such as virtual fitness classes or meditation sessions.

9. Seek Feedback and Act on it:

- **Regular Surveys:** Conduct regular surveys to gather feedback from employees about their engagement and satisfaction in the hybrid work environment.

- **Act on Feedback:** Use the feedback received to make improvements and address any challenges faced by employees in the hybrid work setup.

Conclusion:

Nurturing employee engagement in a hybrid workforce involves creating an inclusive and supportive environment where remote and in-office employees feel connected and valued. By promoting communication, collaboration, recognition, and work-life balance, organizations can build a strong sense of camaraderie and boost productivity among all team members. The key is to embrace the unique opportunities and challenges of the hybrid work model and prioritize employee engagement as a fundamental aspect of the company's success.

Adapting Leadership Styles for Remote and Hybrid Work:

Inspiring and Motivating Teams from a Distance.

Adapting leadership styles for remote and hybrid work is essential for effectively inspiring and motivating teams from a distance. Different work models require different approaches to leadership to ensure team cohesion, productivity, and engagement. Here are strategies to adapt leadership styles for remote and hybrid work environments:

1. Embrace Transformational Leadership:

- **Vision and Inspiration:** Communicate a clear and compelling vision for the team's goals and the organization's mission. Inspire team members by illustrating how their contributions contribute to the bigger picture.

- **Individualized Support:** Provide personalized support and guidance to team members based on their unique strengths, challenges, and career aspirations.

- **Encourage Innovation:** Foster a culture of innovation by encouraging remote and in-office employees to share their ideas and experiment with new approaches.

2. Foster Open and Transparent Communication:

- **Active Listening:** Practice active listening to understand the concerns and feedback of remote employees. Encourage open dialogue and make team members feel heard and valued.

- **Regular Check-ins:** Conduct frequent one-on-one check-ins with remote team members to build a strong rapport and address any issues promptly.

- **Transparent Decision-Making:** Be transparent in decision-making processes and communicate the rationale behind decisions to build trust and reduce uncertainty.

3. Empower and Trust Remote Employees:

- **Autonomy and Ownership:** Provide remote employees with a sense of ownership over their work by empowering them to make decisions and take initiative.

- **Results-Oriented Approach:** Focus on outcomes rather than micromanaging the process. Trust employees to achieve their goals, regardless of their physical location.

4. Facilitate Collaboration and Team Bonding:

- **Virtual Team-Building:** Organize virtual team-building activities and social events that promote camaraderie among remote and in-office team members.

- **Cross-Functional Projects:** Encourage collaboration between different departments or teams to foster a sense of unity and shared purpose.

5. Lead by Example:

- **Work-Life Balance:** Demonstrate the importance of work-life balance by setting boundaries and promoting wellness for both remote and in-office employees.

- **Tech Savviness:** Exhibit proficiency in using remote collaboration tools and technologies, setting an example for the team to follow.

6. Adapt Recognition and Rewards:

- **Virtual Recognition:** Celebrate achievements and recognize outstanding performance virtually to include remote employees in the recognition process.

- **Rewards and Incentives:** Offer rewards and incentives that are accessible to all team members, regardless of their physical location.

7. Provide Remote-Friendly Professional Development:

- **Virtual Training:** Offer virtual training and development opportunities to remote employees to support their career growth and skill enhancement.

- **Mentorship Programs:** Facilitate virtual mentorship programs that connect remote employees with experienced mentors within the organization.

8. Monitor and Support Employee Well-Being:

- **Wellness Initiatives:** Implement wellness programs and initiatives that cater to both remote and in-office employees' well-being.

- **Mental Health Support:** Provide resources and support for remote employees' mental health, acknowledging the potential challenges of remote work.

9. Adapt Leadership Practices Based on Feedback:

- **Seek Feedback Regularly:** Gather feedback from the team, both remote and in-office, about their experiences and needs in the hybrid work environment.

- **Continuously Improve:** Act on the feedback received and make adjustments to leadership practices to better support the team's engagement and performance.

Conclusion:

Adapting leadership styles for remote and hybrid work involves embracing transformational leadership, fostering open communication, empowering remote employees, facilitating collaboration, and leading by example. By prioritizing open communication, inclusivity, and trust, leaders can effectively inspire and motivate teams from a distance. Additionally, recognizing and addressing the unique challenges and opportunities presented by remote and hybrid work models will contribute to building a thriving and engaged workforce in the modern work landscape.

Hybrid Workspaces:

Designing Physical Offices to Accommodate Flexible Work Arrangements.

Hybrid workspaces are physical office environments designed to accommodate flexible work arrangements, where employees have the option to work both remotely and in the office. These workspaces are tailored to support collaboration, connectivity, and productivity, regardless of where team members are located. Here are key aspects to consider when designing hybrid workspaces:

1. Flexible Seating Arrangements:

- **Hot Desking:** Implement a hot-desking system, where employees can choose their workstations each day. This promotes flexibility and encourages employees to come into the office when needed.

- **Activity-Based Spaces:** Create various work zones, such as quiet areas for focused work, collaborative spaces for team meetings, and informal lounges for casual interactions.

2. Technology Integration:

- **Collaboration Tools:** Install video conferencing equipment and large screens in meeting rooms to facilitate seamless communication with remote team members.

- **Cloud-Based Systems:** Integrate cloud-based collaboration tools and project management platforms to ensure easy access to files and information regardless of location.

3. Ergonomic Design:

- **Adjustable Furniture:** Provide ergonomic chairs and adjustable desks to support employee comfort and productivity during extended periods of work.

- **Natural Lighting:** Incorporate ample natural lighting into the workspace design, as it enhances employee well-being and productivity.

4. Prioritize Connectivity:

- **Reliable Internet Access:** Ensure strong and secure internet connectivity throughout the office to support remote communication and collaboration.

- **Wi-Fi Zones:** Establish designated Wi-Fi zones, allowing employees to work wirelessly from various locations within the office.

5. Hybrid Meeting Spaces:

- **Virtual Meeting Rooms:** Set up dedicated meeting rooms equipped with video conferencing technology for seamless virtual collaboration.

- **Digital Whiteboards:** Install digital whiteboards that enable remote employees to participate in brainstorming sessions and visualize ideas in real-time.

6. Wellness and Breakout Spaces:

- **Quiet Zones:** Designate quiet spaces where employees can focus on deep work without distractions.

- **Wellness Rooms:** Create wellness rooms for relaxation, meditation, or nursing, promoting employee well-being.

- **Social Areas:** Incorporate social spaces like communal kitchens or game rooms to foster team bonding and informal interactions.

7. Safety Measures:

- **Health Protocols:** Implement health and safety protocols to ensure the well-being of employees in the office, such as regular cleaning, sanitization, and social distancing measures.

- **Flexible Workspace:** Allow employees to choose their workspace to maintain social distancing and adhere to safety guidelines.

8. Hybrid Work Policies and Guidelines:

- **Clear Policies:** Establish clear hybrid work policies that outline expectations for office attendance, remote work arrangements, and communication protocols.

- **Remote Work Equipment:** Provide remote employees with necessary equipment, such as laptops and peripherals, to support their work from various locations.

9. Continuous Improvement:

- **Gather Employee Feedback:** Regularly seek feedback from employees on their experiences in the hybrid workspace and use it to make improvements.

- **Adapt and Evolve:** Be flexible in adapting the office design and policies based on changing needs and feedback from employees.

Conclusion:

Designing hybrid workspaces requires careful consideration of flexibility, technology integration, connectivity, employee comfort, and safety. A well-designed hybrid workspace supports a seamless transition between in-office and remote work, fosters collaboration, and enhances employee productivity and satisfaction. By prioritizing the needs of both remote and in-office employees, organizations can create a dynamic and inclusive work environment that accommodates flexible work arrangements and supports the success of hybrid work models.

Measuring Success in a Hybrid Work Model:

KPIs and Metrics for Performance Evaluation.

Measuring success in a hybrid work model requires a thoughtful approach to performance evaluation that considers both quantitative and qualitative factors. Key Performance Indicators (KPIs) and metrics should be chosen to assess individual and team performance, as well as the overall effectiveness of the hybrid work model. Here are some essential KPIs and metrics for measuring success in a hybrid work model:

1. Individual Performance Metrics:

- **Output and Productivity:** Measure the quantity and quality of work completed by each employee. This can include the number of tasks completed, projects delivered, or sales generated.

- **Meeting Deadlines:** Assess employees' ability to meet deadlines and deliver work on time.

- **Customer Satisfaction:** If applicable, track customer satisfaction scores and feedback for employees who directly interact with clients or customers.

2. Collaboration and Team Metrics:

- **Team Productivity:** Measure the overall productivity of teams or departments in the hybrid work model.

- **Team Communication:** Assess the effectiveness of team communication, looking at response times, frequency of collaboration, and clarity of communication.

- **Cross-Functional Collaboration:** Evaluate the degree of collaboration and knowledge-sharing between different teams or departments.

3. Employee Engagement and Satisfaction:

- **Employee Surveys:** Conduct regular surveys to gauge employee satisfaction, engagement, and their experiences in the hybrid work model.

- **Retention Rate:** Monitor employee retention to assess how well the hybrid work model meets employee needs and promotes job satisfaction.

- **Feedback and Recognition:** Track the frequency and quality of feedback and recognition provided to employees.

4. Performance Reviews and Goal Achievement:

- **Performance Evaluation:** Evaluate employee performance based on pre-defined goals and objectives.

- **Goal Achievement:** Measure the percentage of set goals that employees successfully achieve during specific periods.

- **Performance Improvement:** Track the progress of employees who have set performance improvement plans.

5. Attendance and Punctuality:

- **Office Attendance:** For in-office employees, measure their attendance and adherence to core working hours.

- **Virtual Presence:** Assess remote employees' virtual presence and availability during core hours.

6. Customer or Client Metrics:

- **Customer Retention:** Measure the retention rate of existing customers or clients.

- **Customer Feedback:** Collect and analyze customer feedback, reviews, and ratings.

- **Customer Acquisition:** If applicable, monitor the rate of new customer acquisition and sales growth.

7. Work-Life Balance and Well-Being:

- **Well-Being Surveys:** Conduct surveys to assess employee well-being and work-life balance.

- **Employee Burnout:** Monitor indicators of burnout, such as increased absenteeism or decreased productivity.

8. Costs and Savings:

- **Cost of Remote Work Setup:** Calculate the cost savings achieved by adopting a hybrid work model.

- **Office Space Utilization:** Measure the efficiency of office space utilization and potential savings on real estate costs.

9. Adoption and Utilization of Technology:

- **Technology Usage:** Monitor the adoption and usage of remote collaboration tools, project management platforms, and other technologies that support hybrid work.

- **Training Completion:** Measure the completion rate of training programs aimed at enhancing remote work skills.

Conclusion:

Measuring success in a hybrid work model requires a comprehensive approach that considers individual performance, team collaboration, employee engagement, customer satisfaction, and overall business outcomes. By selecting the right mix of KPIs and metrics, organizations can evaluate the effectiveness of their hybrid work model, identify areas for improvement, and make data-driven decisions to optimize team performance and employee satisfaction in the evolving work landscape.

Legal and Compliance Considerations for Remote and Hybrid Work:

Addressing Employment and Data Security Issues.

Legal and compliance considerations are crucial when implementing remote and hybrid work models to ensure that the organization operates within the boundaries of applicable laws and regulations. Addressing employment and data security issues is of utmost importance to protect both the company and its employees. Here are some key legal and compliance considerations for remote and hybrid work:

1. Employment Contracts and Agreements:

- **Remote Work Policy:** Clearly outline the terms and conditions of remote work in a comprehensive remote work policy. This should include expectations, working hours, equipment provision, and guidelines for remote employees.

- **Amend Employment Contracts:** Review and amend employment contracts to include provisions related to remote or hybrid work arrangements.

- **State and International Laws:** Ensure compliance with employment laws in different states or countries where remote employees are located.

2. Wage and Hour Compliance:

- **Overtime and Breaks:** Comply with wage and hour laws, including overtime requirements and mandatory break periods for remote and hybrid employees.

- **Tracking Work Hours:** Implement reliable systems for tracking remote employees' work hours to ensure accurate payment for hours worked.

3. Data Security and Privacy:

- **Data Protection Policies:** Establish data protection policies that outline the measures taken to protect sensitive company and customer data.

- **Encryption and Secure Connections:** Require the use of encryption and secure connections when accessing company systems or handling sensitive data remotely.

- **Data Access Permissions:** Limit access to sensitive data based on the principle of least privilege to reduce the risk of data breaches.

4. Cybersecurity Measures:

- **Secure Devices:** Enforce the use of company-issued devices with updated security software for remote work.

- **Security Awareness Training:** Provide cybersecurity training to remote employees to educate them about potential risks and best practices.

- **Incident Response Plan:** Develop an incident response plan to address data breaches or security incidents promptly.

5. Employee Health and Safety:

- **Ergonomic Standards:** Provide guidelines for setting up a safe and ergonomic remote workspace to prevent work-related injuries.

- **Worker's Compensation:** Clarify the process for filing worker's compensation claims for work-related injuries that occur at home.

6. Tax and Payroll Compliance:

- **Tax Implications:** Understand the tax implications for remote employees working in different states or countries and comply with tax laws accordingly.

- **Payroll Compliance:** Ensure accurate payroll processing, considering deductions and tax withholding for remote employees based on their work location.

7. International Employment Laws:

- **Work Permits and Visas:** Ensure that employees working in a different country have the necessary work permits and visas, complying with local employment laws.

- **Social Security Contributions:** Comply with social security contribution requirements for employees working abroad.

8. Record-Keeping and Documentation: Documenting Remote Work

- **Arrangements:** Maintain comprehensive records of remote work agreements, policies, and any changes made to employment contracts.

- **Training Documentation:** Keep records of remote employee training and acknowledgment of cybersecurity and data protection policies.

Conclusion:

Addressing legal and compliance considerations is crucial when implementing remote and hybrid work models. By having clear policies, ensuring data security and privacy, and complying with employment laws and tax regulations, organizations can create a secure and legally compliant remote and hybrid work environment. Regular review and updates to policies and agreements are necessary to adapt to changing laws and regulations and maintain a safe and compliant work environment for both the company and its remote and hybrid employees.

The Future of Work:

Predictions for Remote and Hybrid Models Beyond 2023.

1. Hybrid Work Becomes the Norm: The hybrid work model is likely to become the prevailing work arrangement for many companies. Businesses will continue to embrace the benefits of flexibility and improved work-life balance for employees, while also leveraging in-person collaboration and team-building in physical office spaces.

2. Advanced Remote Collaboration Tools: Technology will play a significant role in enhancing remote collaboration. We can expect to see more advanced virtual reality (VR) and augmented reality (AR) tools that enable a more immersive and interactive remote work experience.

3. Greater Emphasis on Employee Well-Being: Employers will place increased importance on employee well-being and mental health. Companies will invest in wellness programs and initiatives to support the physical and emotional well-being of their remote and hybrid workforce.

4. Customized Work Arrangements: Companies will likely offer more customized work arrangements to suit individual employee preferences. This may include options for working from different locations, flexible hours, and personalized work setups.

5. Shift in Corporate Real Estate: The adoption of hybrid work models may lead to a reevaluation of corporate real estate strategies. Some organizations may downsize office spaces and invest in flexible co-working spaces to accommodate employees who come into the office occasionally.

6. Evolving Leadership Styles:
Leadership practices will continue to evolve to effectively manage and inspire remote and hybrid teams. Leaders will focus on building trust, fostering open communication, and developing a strong virtual team culture.

7. Cybersecurity and Data Protection:
With an increase in remote work, cybersecurity and data protection will be paramount. Companies will invest more in securing remote access and protecting sensitive information to prevent cyber threats.

8. Remote Talent Acquisition: The ability to hire talent from anywhere in the world will become more prevalent, as companies adapt to remote work and recruit employees based on skills and expertise rather than location.

9. Greater Flexibility in Employment Law: Employment laws and regulations will likely adapt to accommodate the changing nature of work. Governments may introduce more flexible policies to support remote and hybrid work arrangements.

10. Continuous Learning and Upskilling: To adapt to a dynamic work environment, employees will be encouraged to engage in continuous learning and upskilling to remain competitive and relevant in their roles.

11. Environmental Impact Considerations: As remote work reduces commuting and office-related activities, companies may place greater emphasis on the environmental impact of their operations, leading to more sustainable practices.

12. Enhanced Employee Experience Platforms: Companies will invest in digital employee experience platforms that provide comprehensive support for remote and hybrid employees, offering seamless access to resources, communication channels, and feedback mechanisms.

Conclusion:

The future of remote and hybrid work beyond 2023 is likely to be shaped by continued advancements in technology, changing workplace norms, and an increased focus on employee well-being and flexibility. As the workforce and business landscape continue to evolve, organizations will need to adapt their strategies and practices to leverage the opportunities presented by remote and hybrid work models.

Remote Work and the Gig Economy:

Exploring the Intersection and Implications for Businesses.

Remote work and the gig economy are two significant trends that have gained prominence in the modern workforce. While they are distinct concepts, they do intersect in certain aspects, and their combination has implications for businesses. Let's explore each concept and then delve into the intersection and implications:

Remote Work:

Remote work refers to the practice of employees working outside the traditional office setting, typically from their homes or other remote locations. Advancements in technology, such as high-speed internet and collaboration tools, have made remote work more feasible and popular. Remote work offers several benefits, including increased flexibility, improved work-life balance, access to a global talent pool, and reduced commuting costs.

The Gig Economy:

The gig economy is characterized by a workforce that consists of independent contractors, freelancers, and temporary workers who take on short-term projects or gigs rather than holding traditional full-time positions. Gig workers are often hired on a per-project basis, allowing businesses to tap into specialized skills as and when needed. The gig economy provides workers with flexibility and autonomy, and it allows businesses to access a diverse talent pool without committing to long-term employment contracts.

Intersection and Implications for Businesses:

1. **Flexible Workforce:** The intersection of remote work and the gig economy enables businesses to build a flexible and agile workforce. They can hire gig workers for specific projects, and these freelancers can work remotely, offering businesses the ability to quickly scale up or down based on project demands.

2. **Access to Global Talent:** The combination of remote work and the gig economy opens up access to a vast global talent pool. Businesses can hire skilled professionals from around the world, regardless of geographical constraints, allowing for greater diversity and expertise in their teams.

3. **Cost Savings:** By employing gig workers for specific projects and

allowing them to work remotely, businesses can save on overhead costs associated with traditional office spaces and benefits for full-time employees.

4. **Skills On-Demand:** The gig economy allows businesses to tap into specialized skills on-demand. They can hire experts for short-term projects without the need to maintain a full-time staff with those specific skills.

5. **Challenges in Collaboration:** While remote work and the gig economy offer flexibility, they can also present challenges in collaboration. With team members working remotely and on different projects, maintaining strong team cohesion and effective communication becomes crucial.

6. **Data Security and Compliance:**
When working with gig workers
remotely, businesses need to consider
data security and compliance issues.
Proper measures must be in place to
protect sensitive company and
customer data, especially when
sharing information with external
contractors.

7. **Employment Classification:** The
gig economy has raised debates about
the classification of workers as
independent contractors vs.
employees. Businesses must navigate
legal and regulatory requirements to
ensure that they are compliant with
labor laws in their region.

8. **Building a Remote Work
Culture:** Businesses need to create a
strong remote work culture that
fosters collaboration, engagement,

and a sense of belonging for both remote employees and gig workers.

9. **Upskilling and Onboarding:** To make the most of the gig economy and remote work, businesses may need to invest in upskilling and onboarding programs to quickly integrate gig workers into the team and ensure they have the necessary skills to contribute effectively.

Conclusion:

The intersection of remote work and the gig economy presents exciting opportunities for businesses to build flexible, diverse, and specialized teams. However, it also comes with challenges related to collaboration, data security, and compliance. Businesses that navigate these implications thoughtfully and embrace the changing nature of work can leverage the benefits of the gig economy and remote work to drive innovation and competitiveness in the modern workforce.

Hybrid Learning and Development Programs:

Upskilling and Training Remote Employees for the Future.

Hybrid learning and development programs combine traditional in-person training with online or remote learning opportunities to upskill and train remote employees for the future. As more businesses embrace remote and hybrid work models, investing in the professional development of remote employees becomes essential to enhance their skills and adapt to evolving job demands. Here's an in-depth explanation of hybrid learning and development programs:

1. Online Learning Platforms:

- **E-Learning Courses:** Offer a wide range of e-learning courses covering various topics and skills. These courses can be accessed remotely, allowing employees to learn at their own pace and convenience.

- **Virtual Workshops and Webinars:** Conduct virtual workshops and webinars facilitated by subject matter experts. Remote employees can participate in live sessions and engage in discussions with trainers and other learners.

2. Virtual Training Sessions:

- **Interactive Sessions:** Utilize video conferencing and virtual collaboration tools to conduct interactive training sessions where remote employees can actively participate in discussions, group activities, and role-playing exercises.

- **Real-Time Feedback:** Provide real-time feedback and support to remote learners during virtual training sessions to address their questions and concerns effectively.

3. Blended Learning Approach:

- **Mix of Modalities:** Employ a blend of online and in-person learning methods to cater to different learning preferences and optimize knowledge retention.

- **Practical Application:** Incorporate hands-on exercises and projects, allowing remote employees to apply their newly acquired skills in real-world scenarios.

4. On-Demand Learning Resources:

- **Learning Libraries:** Create digital learning libraries or knowledge repositories that remote employees can access anytime to review training materials, resources, and job aids.

- **Microlearning:** Offer bite-sized, focused learning modules that can be consumed on-demand, making it easier for remote employees to fit learning into their schedules.

5. Individualized Learning Paths:

- **Skills Assessments:** Conduct skills assessments to identify the specific learning needs of remote employees and tailor their learning paths accordingly.

- **Personalized Learning:** Offer personalized learning paths based on employee performance, career goals, and areas for improvement.

6. Peer Learning and Collaborative Learning:

- **Virtual Study Groups:** Facilitate virtual study groups where remote employees can collaborate, share knowledge, and learn from each other.

- **Mentorship Programs:** Establish mentorship programs that connect remote employees with experienced mentors for personalized guidance and support.

7. Gamified Learning:

- **Gamification Elements:** Integrate gamification elements, such as quizzes, badges, and leaderboards, to make learning engaging and encourage healthy competition among remote employees.

- **Reward and Recognition:** Provide rewards or recognition for completing training milestones and achieving learning objectives.

8. Continuous Learning Culture:

- **Encourage Lifelong Learning:** Foster a culture of continuous learning where remote employees are encouraged to take ownership of their professional development.

- **Leadership Support:** Ensure that leadership actively supports and promotes the value of ongoing learning and upskilling.

9. Evaluating Training Effectiveness:

- **Assessment and Feedback:** Use assessments, quizzes, and surveys to gather feedback from remote employees on the effectiveness of the training programs.

- **Monitoring Performance Improvement:** Track and monitor the performance improvement of remote employees after completing training to measure the impact of learning initiatives.

Conclusion:

Hybrid learning and development programs are valuable tools to upskill and train remote employees for the future. By blending online and in-person learning methods, offering on-demand resources, and promoting a continuous learning culture, businesses can empower their remote workforce to thrive in an ever-changing work environment. Investing in the professional development of remote employees not only enhances their skills but also boosts their motivation, engagement,

and overall contribution to the
organization's success.

Remote Recruitment and Onboarding:

Strategies for Hiring and Integrating Talent from Anywhere.

Remote recruitment and onboarding strategies are essential for businesses seeking to hire and integrate talent from anywhere, especially in the context of remote and hybrid work models. These strategies ensure a smooth and effective hiring process and facilitate a seamless onboarding experience for remote employees. Here's an in-depth explanation of remote recruitment and onboarding strategies:

Remote Recruitment Strategies:

1. **Virtual Job Fairs and Events:** Participate in virtual job fairs and

industry-specific events to connect with a diverse pool of candidates from different locations.

2. **Digital Job Postings:** Advertise job openings on online job boards and professional networking platforms to reach a broader audience of potential candidates.

3. **Video Interviews:** Conduct initial and subsequent rounds of interviews via video conferencing to assess candidates' skills, experience, and cultural fit.

4. **Skills Assessments and Tests:** Implement online skills assessments and tests to evaluate candidates' abilities and suitability for the role.

5. **Use of AI and Automation:** Leverage artificial intelligence and automation tools to streamline

candidate sourcing and screening processes.

6. **Remote Work Policy and Culture:** Highlight the organization's remote work policy and remote-friendly culture in job postings to attract remote talent.

7. **Employee Referral Program:** Encourage current employees to refer potential candidates from their professional networks.

8. **Assessment of Remote Work Skills:** During interviews, assess candidates' remote work skills, including communication, time management, and ability to work independently.

Remote Onboarding Strategies:

1. **Digital Documentation and Paperwork:** Use digital tools for completing onboarding documentation, contracts, and other paperwork.

2. **Virtual Orientation Sessions:** Conduct virtual orientation sessions to introduce new employees to the company's culture, values, policies, and procedures.

3. **Technology Setup:** Ensure that remote employees have the necessary technology, hardware, and software to perform their roles effectively.

4. **Onboarding Portals:** Create onboarding portals or platforms that provide remote employees with easy access to relevant information and resources.

5. **Buddy System:** Assign remote employees a "buddy" or mentor within the company to provide guidance and support during the onboarding process.

6. **Introduction to Team and Colleagues:** Organize virtual meet-and-greet sessions for new remote employees to interact with their team members and colleagues.

7. **Training and Development:** Provide remote employees with access to virtual training and development programs to enhance their skills and knowledge.

8. **Scheduled Check-ins:** Schedule regular check-ins with remote employees during the onboarding process to address any questions or concerns.

Hybrid Onboarding for In-Office and Remote Employees:

1. **Inclusive Onboarding Program:** Design an onboarding program that caters to both in-office and remote employees, ensuring a consistent experience for all.

2. **Virtual Team Building:** Incorporate virtual team-building activities to foster a sense of camaraderie and inclusion among all employees.

3. **Mixed Training Formats:** Offer training sessions that accommodate both in-office and remote employees, allowing everyone to participate effectively.

4. **Communication Tools:** Utilize communication tools and platforms

that facilitate seamless collaboration and connectivity for all team members.

Conclusion:

Remote recruitment and onboarding strategies are vital for attracting and integrating talent from anywhere in the world, enabling businesses to leverage the benefits of remote work and build diverse and skilled teams. By using virtual communication tools, emphasizing remote work policies, and providing a comprehensive onboarding experience, companies can set remote employees up for success and ensure they feel welcomed, supported, and engaged from day one. Additionally, adopting inclusive onboarding programs that cater to both in-office and remote employees contributes to fostering a cohesive and collaborative work environment, regardless of physical location.

Balancing Flexibility and Structure in Hybrid Work:

Establishing Guidelines and Policies for Success.

Balancing flexibility and structure in hybrid work is essential for creating a successful and productive work environment that accommodates both remote and in-office employees. The hybrid work model offers the benefits of flexibility while maintaining essential organizational structure and guidelines. Striking the right balance requires establishing clear policies and guidelines that address various aspects of work. Here's an in-depth explanation:

1. Remote Work Policy:

- Clearly define the eligibility criteria for remote work and the process for requesting remote work arrangements.

- Specify expectations for remote work, including working hours, availability for communication, and reporting requirements.

- Establish guidelines for remote employees' workspace setup, equipment provision, and data security measures.

2. Core Office Hours:

- Set core office hours when all employees are expected to be available for collaboration and meetings.

- Allow flexibility in starting and ending work hours to accommodate diverse employee needs.

3. Communication Guidelines:

- Define preferred communication channels for different types of communication (e.g., team meetings, one-on-one discussions, urgent matters).

- Encourage regular check-ins and ensure remote employees have equal opportunities to participate in discussions.

4. Task and Project Management:

- Utilize project management tools to assign tasks, track progress, and set deadlines for remote and in-office employees.

- Promote transparency by providing access to project updates and ensuring clear communication on responsibilities.

5. Performance Evaluation:

- Develop performance evaluation criteria that consider both in-office and remote employees' contributions and outcomes.

- Focus on results and outcomes rather than the specific location of work.

6. Flexibility for In-Office Employees:

- Offer in-office employees the flexibility to work remotely occasionally, if desired, to experience the benefits of hybrid work.

7. Inclusivity and Engagement:

- Implement inclusive practices that ensure remote employees are actively involved in team activities and decision-making processes.

- Organize team-building events that accommodate both remote and in-office employees.

8. Technology and Connectivity:

- Invest in reliable and user-friendly collaboration tools to enable seamless communication and collaboration for all employees.

- Ensure that remote employees have access to the same level of technological support as in-office employees.

9. Training and Upskilling:

- Provide training programs and resources to help employees adapt to the hybrid work model and enhance their remote work skills.

- Encourage continuous learning to support employee growth and development.

10. Wellness and Work-Life Balance:

- Promote work-life balance by encouraging employees to set boundaries and take breaks.

- Offer wellness programs that cater to the well-being of both remote and in-office employees.

11. Feedback and Adaptation:

- Regularly seek feedback from employees regarding the hybrid work model's effectiveness and areas for improvement.

- Use feedback to adapt policies and guidelines to better support the needs of the workforce.

12. Manager Training:

- Provide training to managers to effectively lead and support hybrid teams.

- Train managers on how to foster team cohesion, set clear expectations, and offer remote employees the same opportunities as in-office employees.

Conclusion:

Balancing flexibility and structure in a hybrid work model requires thoughtful planning and the establishment of clear guidelines and policies. By providing flexibility for remote work while maintaining essential organizational structure, businesses can create an environment where both in-office and remote employees can thrive. The success of the hybrid work model hinges on effective communication, inclusive practices, and a focus on results and outcomes rather than the physical location of work. Regular feedback and adaptation of policies will help optimize the hybrid work experience and support the organization's goals and the well-being of its employees.

Mental Health and Remote Work:

Supporting Employees' Well-being in a Distributed Workforce.

Supporting employees' mental health is crucial in any work environment, and it becomes even more significant in a remote or distributed workforce where employees may face unique challenges and isolation. Here's an in-depth explanation of how to address mental health and support employees' well-being in a remote work setting:

1. Promote Open Communication:

- Encourage regular check-ins between managers and remote employees to discuss work progress, challenges, and well-being.

- Create a culture of open communication where employees feel comfortable expressing their concerns and seeking support.

2. Set Clear Expectations and Boundaries:

- Clearly communicate work expectations, deadlines, and availability to minimize stress and anxiety related to workloads.

- Encourage employees to set boundaries between work and personal life, such as defining specific work hours and taking breaks.

3. Virtual Social Interaction:

- Organize virtual team-building activities, social events, and informal gatherings to foster a sense of camaraderie and combat feelings of isolation.

- Promote virtual coffee breaks or lunch sessions where employees can connect and chat casually.

4. Mental Health Resources:

- Provide access to mental health resources, such as employee assistance programs (EAPs), counseling services, or mental health apps.

- Offer information and educational materials on coping with stress, burnout, and maintaining a healthy work-life balance.

5. Flexible Work Arrangements:

- Offer flexibility in work schedules to accommodate employees' personal needs and responsibilities, which can reduce stress and promote work-life balance.

6. Encourage Physical Well-being:

- Promote regular physical activity and provide resources for at-home workouts or virtual fitness classes.

- Advocate for regular breaks during the workday to stretch and move around to reduce sedentary behavior.

7. Mental Health Training for Managers:

- Train managers to recognize signs of stress and mental health issues and provide them with the tools to support their team members effectively.

- Foster a supportive and empathetic management style that encourages employees to share their concerns.

8. Combating Isolation:

- Encourage virtual team collaboration and communication to prevent feelings of isolation.

- Establish virtual "watercooler" channels where employees can chat casually and share non-work-related updates.

9. Recognize and Appreciate:

- Acknowledge and appreciate employees' efforts and accomplishments regularly to boost morale and motivation.

- Recognize the challenges remote work may bring and show empathy and understanding.

10. Addressing Workload and Burnout:

- Monitor workloads and ensure that they are reasonable and manageable for remote employees.

- Address signs of burnout promptly and provide necessary support, such as workload adjustments or time off.

11. Workshops and Webinars:

- Organize workshops and webinars on mental health, stress management, and resilience to empower employees with coping strategies.

12. Employee Well-being Surveys:

- Conduct regular employee well-being surveys to gather feedback and identify areas of concern to tailor support programs.

Conclusion:

Supporting employees' mental health in a remote work environment requires a proactive and holistic approach. By fostering open communication, promoting social interactions, providing mental health resources, and recognizing the challenges of remote work, organizations can create a supportive work culture that prioritizes employees' well-being. Implementing strategies to combat isolation, address workloads, and support work-life balance will not only enhance the mental health of employees but also lead to increased productivity, engagement, and overall job satisfaction in a distributed workforce.

Hybrid Work and Environmental Sustainability:

Reducing Carbon Footprints Through Remote Models.

Hybrid work models have the potential to positively impact environmental sustainability by reducing carbon footprints and promoting more eco-friendly work practices. Here's an in-depth explanation of how hybrid work can contribute to environmental sustainability:

1. Reduced Commuting Emissions:

- By allowing employees to work remotely part of the time, hybrid work models significantly reduce commuting emissions. Fewer people driving or using public transportation to the office means less greenhouse gas emissions from vehicles, leading to a decreased carbon footprint.

2. Energy Savings in Office Spaces:

- With a portion of the workforce working remotely, there is reduced demand for office spaces. This leads to energy savings in buildings, including reduced electricity usage for lighting, heating, and cooling.

3. Lower Resource Consumption:

- Hybrid work models result in decreased resource consumption in office spaces. Fewer employees in the office mean less water usage, paper consumption, and other resources typically associated with office operations.

4. Decreased Business Travel:

- In a hybrid work environment, virtual meetings and remote collaboration tools become more prevalent, reducing the need for extensive business travel. This results in fewer flights and less fuel consumption, leading to lower carbon emissions from business travel.

5. Flexible Workspaces:

- Hybrid work models encourage the use of flexible workspaces, such as coworking spaces or satellite offices, instead of a centralized office location. These flexible spaces often adopt more sustainable practices, such as energy-efficient lighting and recycling programs.

6. Remote Work Technology:

- The adoption of remote work technology allows employees to collaborate virtually, reducing the need for physical meetings and unnecessary travel. Utilizing virtual communication tools and video conferencing platforms minimizes the environmental impact of business operations.

7. Eco-Conscious Behavior:

- Remote work can encourage employees to adopt more eco-conscious behavior in their personal lives. Being at home more often may lead to increased awareness of energy usage, waste reduction, and sustainable practices in their households.

8. Supporting Green Initiatives:

- Companies implementing hybrid work models can align their sustainability goals by incorporating green initiatives into their remote work policies. Encouraging eco-friendly practices among remote employees can have a broader positive impact.

9. Carbon Offsetting:

- Companies can choose to invest in carbon offsetting initiatives to further reduce their carbon footprints. These initiatives involve funding projects that help offset the company's carbon emissions, such as reforestation or renewable energy projects.

10. Sustainable Work Practices:

- Promoting sustainable work practices among remote employees, such as recycling, energy conservation, and paperless workflows, can contribute to environmental sustainability.

Conclusion:

Hybrid work models have the potential to create a positive impact on environmental sustainability by reducing commuting emissions, lowering resource consumption in office spaces, and decreasing business travel. By embracing remote work technology and supporting eco-conscious behavior among employees, companies can further contribute to reducing their carbon footprints. Incorporating sustainable practices into remote work policies and investing in carbon offsetting initiatives demonstrate a commitment to environmental sustainability and create a more eco-friendly and responsible approach to work operations. Overall, hybrid work models provide an opportunity for businesses to take meaningful steps towards a more sustainable future.